THE SECRET OF THE
EMERALD TABLET

Dr. Gottlieb Latz

Translated by D. William Hauck

The Alchemical Press

THE SECRET OF THE EMERALD TABLET – Copyright © 1992, 1996 by Holmes Publishing Group and D. William Hauck (translator). All rights reserved. No part of this book may be reproduced or utilized in any form or by any means, electronic or mechanical, including photocopying, recording or by any information storage and retrieval system, without permission in writing from Holmes Publishing Group except in the case of brief quotations embodied in critical articles and reviews.

ISBN # 1-55818-203-9

Second Edition

HOLMES PUBLISHING GROUP LLC
POSTAL BOX 2370
SEQUIM WA 98382 USA

Translator's Preface

The first decision made by any translator is whether to try to convey the period and writing style of an author or to concentrate on making his meaning clear to modern readers. It soon became obvious, due to the length and complexity of this work, that I had to choose the latter method. I am sure the author would agree with my decision, because above all else, Dr. Gottlieb Latz was a man of ideas.

His monumental work, *Die Alchemie*, was published in Bonn in 1869. The book is divided into 131 chapters, totaling nearly 600 pages, which trace the history of alchemy through fifty centuries. The present translation is taken from Dr. Latz' research concerning the first three Greek revisions of the Emerald Tablet. All three of these documents were written in Alexandria before the birth of Christ.

Dr. Latz began his exhaustive study of alchemy in hopes of helping his patients. He believed that the secret Elixir of Life was known by the ancient alchemists, but was lost through centuries of conflict and persecution. He tried to reconstruct the formula of the Elixir by careful study of alchemical texts, in particular the mysterious Emerald Tablet of Hermes. He was so sure of his success, that he used his alchemical compounds on many of his patients, who responded favorably to his treatments.

What is more, Dr. Latz, like many alchemists before him, saw in the chemistry of the Arcanum a profound allegory of the formation and evolution of the universe. Along the way in his practical search for the Universal Cure, this nineteenth century genius rediscovered the Shining Light of Truth in one of the oldest documents of mankind.

D. William Hauck, 1993

Foreword

My professors taught me: *Qui bene diagnosit, bene medebitur* (the better the diagnosis, the better the cure). The perverse falsehood of this saying lies right before our eyes! As doctors, we are very capable in our diagnostic talents, but our ability to cure lags far behind. We know how to recognize malignant tumors, pneumonia, syphilis, meningitis, pox, cholera, arthritis, angina—the list goes on and on. But all we can do is watch as our patients suffer.

There are many illnesses in the gray area between curable and incurable that give us the opportunity to get rid of all our illusions. Medicine used to believe any disease was curable. That was because thousands of years ago, physicians had knowledge of alchemy. I became convinced of their knowledge, when I prescribed, out of sheer desperation, a sodium compound mentioned in an old alchemy text. The patient recovered overnight!

Continued experimentation led me to believe that a single-minded, absolutely thorough study of alchemy was necessary. Yet my practice required me to travel the countryside by foot and on horse, day and night, in heat and cold, in dust, rain, hail, and snow to take care of my sick, pregnant, or wounded patients. How could I take up a difficult and consuming study of the ancient Greek and Latin writings of alchemists? I did not see how it would be possible. But gradually there awakened in me a greater dimension that allowed me to handle the workload.

Totally alone I searched to find the Arcanum. First I looked at hundreds of possibilities mentioned by alchemists, then I narrowed my study to one in ten. If it seemed right, I tried it at the sickbeds of my patients, trying to make sense of what dosage to use and how it worked. Finally, with the aid of the Emerald Tablet, I found what I was looking for.

I am the first person who has openly divulged the secrets of the alchemists, because the alchemists themselves tried to conceal their knowledge and did everything they could to entice people down the wrong path. In actual fact, from what they held back, you can follow the thing to its true source.

You cannot imagine how many times my exhausted hand fell away from the pages that lie before you now. But I have completed my goal. You will find herein things that you never would have guessed to be true: that the medical profession is descended from a secret tradition, that we have much in common with the alchemists, that only through the study of alchemy will we find real enlightenment.

Gottlieb Latz
January 1, 1869

Chapter One

The Origin of the Emerald Tablet &
The Ancient Science of Alchemy

Alchemy is the study of the Arcanum and how one can obtain it. The Arcanum, also known as the Elixir, Powder, or Stone, is the fundamental secret of nature. It is said to have the ability to perfect anything, to change baser metals into gold, to cure disease, to make man whole.

The search for the Arcanum began in the darkest reaches of antiquity. Indian alchemists called it —Soma— in ancient Vedic texts and concealed its properties in a colorful variety of Gods. The Chinese sought for it in the form of a Pill of Immortality. Islamic alchemists referred to it as Rasayana. It was traced back to the first day of creation by Judaic alchemists. Greek philosophers saw it everywhere in nature, hidden in the composition of all matter. But it was the Egyptians who made it a science.

The ideas of alchemy were incorporated into all levels of Egyptian culture. It was their practical science, as well as their religion. An Egyptian sage known as Hermes Trismegistus is said to have written thousands of books on alchemy and other topics. Although some of his works were kept in secret by priests, many of his manuscripts were lost when the great world library at Alexandria was burned by Muslims. Only about forty of his works have survived. Nevertheless, he is said to have authored the most important and revered document of alchemy, the *Tabula Smaragdina*, or the Emerald Tablet.

The Emerald Tablet is such an important document that the entire history of alchemy can be divided into the period before the Tablet and the period after. Alchemical thought centered around the interpretation of the Tablet for over 2,000 years. This mysterious communication speaks directly to our intuitive understanding, and the reader feels compelled to search for the deeper meaning of its precepts. The alchemists believed that the secrets of their art were buried in its enigmatic lines.

The origin of the Emerald Tablet has been traced as far back as the biblical Genesis, but most scholars attribute it to Hermes Trismegistus, whose name means Thrice Greatest Hermes or Ruler of the Three Worlds. In all probability, such a person really existed, but it is now impossible to separate the actual person from the legends that identify him with Thoth, the Egyptian god of learning and magic, the inventor of all numbers and science.

Albertus Magnus wrote that Alexander the Great discovered the Tablet at the tomb of Hermes in Phoenicia. Wilhelm Kriegsmann has related a legend that Sarah, wife of Abraham, stumbled upon the Tablet in a cave near Hebron and pried it loose from the stiff fingers of a mummified corpse and other sources allege that Hermes was the son of Adam. Hermes is said to have discovered the Tablet in a cave while traveling in Ceylon, yet some say it was discovered in an underground room of the pyramid of Cheops. Most stories describe the Tablet as a green-colored stone with raised, bas-relief lettering in the Phoenician alphabet.

After extensive and painstaking research into the history of the Emerald Tablet, I discovered that a revised Greek translation of the original text was issued around 300 B.C. This translation was performed by three Alexandrian alchemists, who were attempting to use the mysterious tablet to unify conflicting Jewish, Greek, and Egyptian versions of alchemy.

The mixing of cultures in Alexandria caused a shattering clash of dogmas that shook alchemy to its roots. Because these ideas were treated with such secrecy among the ruling classes, the masses (and history) took little note of the potentially catastrophic nature of the conflict. Even today, it is hard for us to imagine the shattering impact this crisis of interpretation had on the world. Alchemy was considered a gift direct from God. It was the hidden foundation upon which the world's religions and sciences were built. The truths of alchemy were a nation's highest secrets and were revealed only to a small group of worthy priests and philosophers.

The enlightened tone of the Emerald Tablet so effectively defused this explosive situation; it must have been divinely inspired. The creation of the Tablet actually preserved the esoteric basis of Western Civilization. Although the rise of Christianity suppressed the hermetic doctrines, they were passed on to later generations through a variety of occult groups and disciplines.

The Emerald Tablet calls itself the "philosophy of the whole universe," and this is perhaps its most fitting title. However, it was never the nature of alchemists to freely divulge the import of the work, nor to offer the uninitiated such an obvious and tantalizing prize. The original version was probably named *Tabula Smaragdina*, because it was precisely that, a green-colored stone tablet. The first Greek translation and first revision probably went by the same name.

The second revision has been called the *Tabula Hermetica*. More fitting perhaps would be *Tabula Aegyptiaca*, owing to its origins. Most appropriate would be *Tabula Khemica*, a term which reflects the ancient name of Egypt (*kheme* means black soil of the Nile) and the roots of our own science of chemistry. The modern name of alchemy stems from the Arabic Al-Khemi, meaning the "Egyptian science."

The third revision came to be known as the *Tabula de Operatione Solis*. This was a metaphysical interpretation that received wide acceptance and became the driving force behind alchemy through the sixteenth century. In the present work, the author will refer to the Emerald Tablet generally as the Tabula.

Unfortunately, the original Emerald Tablet has not survived. Some legends trace it as far back as Genesis, while other evidence suggests that it was written about 3000 B.C., when the Phoenicians settled on the Syrian coast. The only complete modern text is a very early Latin translation, which exists in three versions. These three Latin versions correspond to the three Greek language revisions of a still older translation of the original Emerald Tablet. All three revisions were written in Alexandria, where Greek was the common tongue. Since neither the original translation nor the original document has survived, we have only the three revisions with which to work.

The history of Alexandria is usually divided into two periods. The first, from 332 B.C. to 30 B.C., is the time of the Ptolemies and the great library. The city was founded by Alexander the Great as a center of Greek culture in Egypt. It quickly inherited the trade of the ancient Phoenician city of Tyre and even passed Carthage in size. The second period runs from 30 B.C. to 638 A.D. The city became part of the Roman Empire during this time; then a center of Christian learning around 300 A.D. It was finally conquered by the Arabs around 640 A.D.

For our purposes, it is convenient to divide the two Alexandrian Periods into three subdivisions, which correspond to the three revisions of the Emerald Tablet. The First Revision was written sometime between 300 B.C. and 270 B.C., because it is based on ideas of the First Alexandrian School, which flourished during that time. The Egyptian and Hellenic cultures were involved in a fruitful merging, and this version reflects their world view. This first version is centered around the three elements of Liquid, Solid, and Air. Fire was considered the agent of change between the elements.

The Second Revision was probably written around 270 B.C., because the Alexandrian Empirical School came into power at that time. Among other things, the Empiricists accepted Fire as a fourth element. By this time the city had also become a center of Semitic scholarship. A Greek version of the Old Testament was being translated there. Specific changes were made in the Second Revision of the *Tabula* that reflected the empirical and Jewish interpretations.

The Third Revision was probably conceived sometime in the period from 50 B.C. to 1 A.D. This metaphysical evaluation suggested that non-physical processes were involved in the transformation of base metals into gold. It was this interpretation that allowed the rise of swindlers, puffers, and fakes, who called themselves alchemists. But it was also with this third interpretation that the ideas of alchemy finally took a form that could be understood by all men, regardless of culture or religion.

It should be mentioned that a fourth interpretation originated in Alexandria around 300 A.D. It stemmed from the Neoplatonic School, which attempted to combine Greek philosophy with Arab mysticism and the moral doctrines of Judaism and Christianity. This rendering did not require another revision of the *Tabula*, but it was the first of many dozens of personal, philosophical, and even prophetic interpretations of the original three revisions.

With the Arab conquest of Egypt in the seventh century, Alexandrian alchemy was passed through Arabian sources (most notably Jabir Hayyan, or Geber). Eventually, knowledge of the art spread to Morocco, and by the eighth century alchemy had taken a strong hold in Spain. The three revisions of the Emerald Tablet found their way to Europe along this same path. That is, the original Greek versions were translated into the Arabic tongue and into Latin. For the next thousand years, alchemy would flourish on the European continent.

Chapter Two

The Ancient Arcana Revealed—The Chemical Arcana

Before we attempt to interpret the meaning of the Emerald Tablet, we must become familiar with some of the chemicals with which the ancient alchemists worked. The existence of these chemicals were considered great secrets (arcana), and their reactions and properties symbolized the basic forces and evolution of the universe. The central tenet of the Tabula was that the microcosm reflected the macrocosm: "As Above, So Below."

The Emerald Tablet is written on many different levels. One of these hidden levels presents a complete description of the chemistry of the Arcanum, the single substance that could produce all the miracles promised by the alchemists. This single Arcanum was made with four chemical compounds: Vitriol, Natron, Pulvis Solaris, and Liquor Hepatis.

The alchemists secured both sulphuric acid and iron from an oily substance that appeared naturally from the weathering of sulphur-bearing gravel. This substance was known as the Green Vitriol, or Iron Vitriol. When it was heated, it broke down into a mixture of iron oxide, iron sulfate, and sulphuric acid. The acid was separated out by distillation.

The acid produced from Green Vitriol is brown and stinks like rotten eggs. Taking the distillation further produces a heavy, nearly odorless, yellow liquid known as Oil of Vitriol. Still further distillation and rectification gives the clear acid, called sulphuricum depuratum or sulphuricum medicinale. Sulphuric acid is a corrosive acid that reacts with most metals (but not gold). It also has a tremendous affinity for water. If a flask of Oil of Vitriol is allowed to stand open, the acid absorbs water vapor from the air and overflows its container. It was considered the agent of change and transformation in most alchemical experiments, and remains an indispensable agent in nearly all modern manufacturing industries.

The Egyptians smelted iron ore as far back as 1500 B.C. They used rust to heal wounds and probably prepared a therapeutic tonic from pure iron sulfate. This was its form when separated from the Green Vitriol during the distillation process to produce sulphuric acid. Green Vitriol in its natural state is a powerful disinfectant.

Iron has long been associated with strength and blood, and many of its compounds are named after Mars, the god of war. Iron ore is extremely abundant in the earth's crust, and its compounds are responsible for most of the green, yellow, brown, and red coloring in rocks.

The word Natron is from the Arabian name for the white salts that accumulate on dry lake beds. The word was used by the alchemists to refer to either one of two sodium compounds. The first of these was Natron carbonicum (soda ash or sodium carbonate), which appears on dried lake beds, forms on the surface of some rocks, or is mined out of the earth. The world's oldest known deposits are in Egypt. Natron carbonicum can also be prepared by pouring sulphuric acid over common table salt. The solution is mixed with lime (calcium oxide produced by heating limestone) and powdered charcoal. After heating, the liquid is poured off, leaving a residue that is allowed to dry. The pure crystals of sodium carbonate can then be isolated.

The second Natron was Natron nitricum, or sodium nitrate. It occurs naturally as cubic-saltpeter (or Chile-saltpeter) and needs only to be refined to be used medicinally. It can also be obtained by pouring Acid of Saltpeter (nitric acid) over common table salt. The alchemists made nitric acid by pouring sulphuric acid over common saltpeter (potassium nitrate). They called the new acid *aqua fortis* and used it to separate silver from gold. In the Natron salt solution, the acid is distilled out and the residue allowed to crystallize. Alchemists sometimes referred to this nitric acid solution as Natron acid.

The alchemists never associated the metal sodium with Natron because of its tendency to immediately form compounds. However, they did suspect an elemental basis for the vast majority of salts that cover the earth. To them, Natron symbolized the common principle in all salts and the formation of bodies in general.

The simplest way to produce Liquor Hepatis is to mix hydrogen sulfide with spirit of ammonia. This method was discovered by later Western alchemists. Ancient alchemists were not familiar with this technique and were forced to prepare the Liquor by distilling a solution of sulphur, lime, and *sal ammoniac* (ammonium chloride). They produced ammonia by gently heating nitrogenous matter (such as camel dung) in sealed containers. The resulting putrefaction produced a variety of ammonia compounds.

Because of its red-brown color, Liquor Hepatis was associated with the liver. The name comes from the Greek word *hepar*, meaning liver. Other obvious characteristics of Liquor Hepatis are its oily consistency and sulphuric content. In fact, some alchemists saw it as a solution of sulphur in oil and called it Oleum sulphuris or Hepar sulphuris.

Liquor Hepatis exuded a pungent odor the alchemists could not account for. They equated this mysterious fragrance with an ethereal presence hidden in the sulphur and lime, and activated by the fertile principle in ammonia. To the ancient alchemists, this fetid odor symbolized the unredeemed soul, a spiritized presence which Egyptians believed resided in the liver. As soul, it could not be broken down any further.

By thickening the Liquor into a balsam, they incorporated this odor into a solid body. Generally, a balsam is made from a fragrant oil, to which is added fat, wax, or honey as a thickening agent. The result is a pasty solid. The balsam of Hepatis came to be known as the Balsam of the Alchemists, or "Balsam of the Soul."

The possibility of materializing a hidden presence into a second body (like a balsam) became a fundamental goal of alchemy. Not only did the Liquor Hepatis contain the principle of the soul, but it suggested the idea of its resurrection, long before it became Christian dogma.

If Liquor Hepatis represented Soul, then Pulvis Solaris represented Spirit. Pulvis Solaris was made up of a mixture of Red Pulvis Solaris and Black Pulvis Solaris. These two Powders of the Sun were created separately by combining sulphur auratum with either red mercuric oxide or black antimony. The unique properties of the Red Pulvis Solaris were to fire the imaginations of alchemists for many hundreds of years.

Mercury was known to the alchemists as quicksilver or the living silver—*Argentum vivum*. It could be found weeping through cracks in rocks or accumulated in small puddles in mountain grottos. By roasting rocks of mercury sulfide (Cinnabar), the shiny metal dripped down into the ashes, from which it was later collected. The red oxide of mercury can be made by heating mercury in a long-necked flask. The mercury is oxidized into a white (poisonous) powder and red (therapeutic) crystals.

The Alexandrians knew of at least one other way. By heating a mixture of mercury and Acid of Saltpeter (nitric acid), a larger quantity of red mercuric oxide was precipitated. This crystalline oxide was dried, rubbed with mercury, and heated once again. Then it was ground fine and washed in distilled water. A very small percentage dissolved in the liquid, which was used for medicinal purposes. The dried red powder, when mixed with sulphur auratum, became Red Pulvis Solaris.

What the alchemists found highly significant in this process was the appearance of a thick red vapor above the surface of the nitric acid. In conjunction with the accumulation below of a red precipitate, this process illustrated the simultaneous separation of mercury into the Above and the Below. Mercury obviously contained the arcanum of both heaven and earth.

The opposing properties of mercury were demonstrated in other compounds. Calomel, or mercury chloride, is a powerful medicine (a liver stimulant and cathartic), unless it is directly exposed to light. In that case, it becomes a deadly poison. Liquid mercury tends to solidify (form amalgams) with other metals. Therefore, quicksilver came to symbolize the god Mercury (or Hermes), who was the god of both heaven and earth, of thresholds and transitions, a guide of souls.

Sulphur was known to the ancients as Brimstone (the burning stone) and was used widely for medicinal purposes. Pure natural sulphur was thought to exist in two varieties: red and white. Sulphur auratum (golden sulphur) was made by first heating a solution of black antimony, sublimated sulphur, sodium carbonate, and milk of lime. The dried mixture is known today as Schlipp's Salt. When sulphuric acid is added to the salt, hydrogen sulfide gas is formed and the sulphur auratum settles to the bottom. This process is similar to the production of red mercuric oxide. Both develop a gas above and a solid precipitate below.

Black antimony is a naturally occurring sulfide of antimony known as Stibnite. The mineral is smelted and ground fine. It was used medicinally by mixing the powder in distilled water. Roasting of the mineral and reduction with powdered charcoal releases the pure metallic antimony. Mixing the finely ground mineral with sulphur auratum produced the Black Pulvis Solaris.

Pulvis Solaris was also known by Western alchemists as the *Bezoardicum*. A bezoar is a concretion sometimes found in the intestines of animals and men. Egyptian priests discovered them during the preparation of animal and human mummies. Bezoars are usually made up of hair, food, or vegetable fiber. At one time, physicians thought the mass protected the body from poisons and actually prescribed it for patients.

However, Egyptian alchemists believed the bezoar was a magical substance formed by the large serpent (the intestines) in man. They even looked for the magical pill in the small serpent (the brain), which looked remarkably like intestines in the head. Since early alchemists associated the serpent with the red mercury precipitate, they also referred to Red Pulvis Solaris as *Pulvis Serpentum*.

Certainly sulphur auratum seems to have an affinity for either red mercuric oxide or black antimony, with which it clumps together immediately. Furthermore, some alchemists believed that red mercuric oxide was somehow naturally produced by snakes, just as black antimony was thought to be produced by plants. They believed that bezoars could be found not only in animals and man, but also in the plant kingdom. In fact, they considered gold to be a mineral bezoar formed in the bowels of the earth.

Alchemists believed color to be an important feature of chemical compounds and sometimes grouped substances by their colors instead of chemical properties. The alchemists associated different colors with specific alchemical qualities, such as the life force (green) or transformative power (red), or the presence of certain metals, such as gold (yellow).

Each arcana had a specific colors associated with it. sulphuric acid was yellow, although in its crudest form brown. Iron was usually associated with the color red, although it imparted a green color to many of its compounds. Sodium carbonate was white, and sodium nitrate was associated with the color blue, the color of Natron acid. Liquor Hepatis was reddish-brown, but it was often associated with the green color of bile. Red Pulvis Solaris was in fact reddish-orange in color, due to the mixture of the red mercuric oxide with yellow sulphur auratum. Similarly, Black Pulvis Solaris was actually of a brown color, due to the mixture of the black antimony with sulphur. The mixture of the Red and Black powders produced Pulvis Solaris, which had an orange-brown color.

Three of the four major arcana actually consist of dual ingredients that are easily separable. Vitriol can be broken down into sulphuric acid and iron. Natron appears as sodium carbonate and sodium nitrate. Pulvis Solaris is used as the Red Pulvis Solaris (mercuric oxide and sulphur) and the Black Pulvis Solaris (antimony sulfide and sulphur). Thus, seven chemicals comprise the ancient arcana: sulphuric acid, Iron, Sodium Carbonate, Sodium Nitrate, Liquor Hepatis, Red Pulvis Solaris, and Black Pulvis Solaris. These were the secret ingredients used in the creation of the mysterious Arcanum. The Emerald Tablet contains encoded instructions on how to combine these compounds in the Arcanum Experiment.

Chapter Three

The First Revision: *The Tabula Smaragdina*

The following is the text of the First Revision of the Emerald Tablet. It was probably written by a Greek or Jew between 300 B.C. and 270 B.C. The original Latin document is divided into four rubrics, in which the initial letters of selected sentences are emphasized in red ink.

Rubric 1: It is true without lie, certain and most true. What is Below is like that which is Above. And that which is Above, like that which is Below, serve to bring the wonder of the Universe into existence. And as all things originate from One thing, from the Idea of One Mind: so do all created things originate from this One thing through adaptation. Its father is the Sun, its mother the Moon. The Wind carried it in its belly, its nurse is the Earth. It is the father of all existing things in the entire Universe. Its inherent virtue is perfected when it is changed into Earth.

Rubric 2: Separate the Earth from the Fire, the Subtle from the Gross, repeatedly with great skillfulness. It rises from Earth to Heaven, and falls back down again to Earth, thereby containing within itself the powers of both the Above and the Below.

Rubric 3: Thus will you obtain the glory of the entire Universe. Every darkness will leave you.

Rubric 4: This is the greatest strength of all, because it conquers every subtle thing and penetrates every solid thing. In this way, was the Universe created. From this proceeds wonders, of which herewith is an example. Therefore, I am called the three-times glorified Hermes, because I possess all three parts of true understanding of the whole Universe. What I have had to say about the operation of the Sun is completed.

The early alchemists were constantly searching for a single phenomena which would illustrate all the basic ideas of their work. The single experiment which most readily demonstrated these principles became known as the Great Secret, or the Arcanum Experiment. The basic experiment required four ingredients, which were called arcana: Liquor Hepatis, Pulvis Solaris, Vitriol, and Natron. Because Liquor Hepatis and Pulvis Solaris united together to produce a moist red vapor, some accounts say there were really only three basic ingredients.

Whether the experiment had three or four ingredients became extremely important in those early days in Alexandria, because each ingredient is described separately in the Emerald Tablet. These ingredients often represented much more than mere chemicals. For example, the mixture of Liquor Hepatis (as soul) with Pulvis Solaris (as spirit) became an underlying theme in alchemy.

Ideally the Arcanum Experiment should succeed on many levels, not only demonstrating the deepest philosophical and psychological principles, but also providing concrete evidence of their veracity. The First Revision of the Emerald Tablet had to be prepared in such a way that all factions could interpret the document according to the foundations of their own faith and philosophy, while at the same time accurately describing the steps in the Arcanum Experiment.

There was a conflict of "ideas" between Greek and Jewish alchemists and one of the major points occurred during the attempts to prepare a unified codex of alchemy was the insistence by the Jewish faction that the *Tabula* should be based on the creation story presented in the Book of Genesis. This was absolutely unacceptable to the Greeks, who believed the *Tabula* should be based on the "great secret of nature" discovered by the ancient Greek philosophers. This was the Principle of the Four Elements, demonstrated many times over in careful experiments by Thales and others.

The Jewish-Greek crisis was resolved only when it was possible for the Jewish alchemists to interpret the ingredients of the Arcanum Experiment in terms of Genesis; namely, that each element corresponded to the subjects of the creation story: Heaven, Earth, and Water. For the Greeks, the ingredients had to correspond to the Four Elements: Air, Water, Earth, and Fire.

We can be sure that the Greek faction at Alexandria pushed for an interpretation of the Emerald Tablet that supported the ideas of Thales, Empedocles, Plato, and Aristotle. Greek alchemy was dominated by the principle of the Four Elements. These elements corresponded to the four states of matter: Air (gases), Water (liquids), Earth (solids), and Fire (the agent or temperature which brings about the transformations of the other three). Fire and Air were viewed as active, masculine elements; Earth and Water were seen as passive, feminine elements. Even human temperament and character were the result of the interaction of the Four Elements within one's personality.

Since the Four Elements were used to explain physical as well as spiritual questions, the hierarchical arrangement of the Elements became extremely important. Fire was the first element and Air the second. This was based on the idea that fire contained air (as smoke), but not all air necessarily contained fire.

Water was placed third and Earth fourth, based on the so-called Water-Transformation experiment. In this demonstration, standing water evaporates and leaves behind mineral deposits. For this reason, the Greeks believed that water contained earth and preceded it.

Thus Fire and Water were seen as the primary elements from which all the universe was created. The superior roles assigned to Fire and Water required that the compounds in the Arcanum Experiment corresponding to them must take superior positions in all reactions. For that reason, the Greeks insisted that the Water arcanum was sulphuric acid and the Earth arcanum was Natron (because it sank to the bottom of the acid). In the same manner, they insisted that the Fire arcanum was Liquor Hepatis and the Air arcanum was Pulvis Solaris, because the powdered Solaris settled to the bottom of the Liquor Hepatis.

Unfortunately, the Greek perspective was in direct opposition to Egyptian and Jewish thinking about the nature of the compounds. Later alchemists and the author's own calculations and experiments suggest the proper assignment should be the Egyptian or Jewish view. That is, Pulver Solaris is the Fire arcanum and Liquor Hepatis is the Air arcanum. Nonetheless, the Greeks found expression for their interpretation of the Arcanum Experiment and the controversy raged among alchemists for centuries.

In the Greek view, the first rubric presented the first pair of compounds in the Arcanum Experiment. From a microcosmic viewpoint, sulphuric acid is "what is Above" and Natron is "what is Below", and they both serve to bring the wonder of this part of the Experiment into existence. At the same time they represent the macrocosmic forces of Water and Earth, respectively. On this level, they serve to bring the wonder of the whole universe into existence.

On the basis of the Water Transformation Experiment and the actual layering of the compounds in the Arcanum Experiment:

Sulphuric Acid = Water = Above = the Superior Element
Natron = Earth = Below = the Inferior Element

The second rubric presents the second pair of compounds in the Arcanum Experiment. In keeping with the principle presented in the previous rubric, the ordering of the pair of compounds in this part of the Experiment should also follow the scheme of Water Above and Earth Below. Based on the controversial designation of the Alexandrian Greeks:

Liquor Hepatis = Water + Fire
Pulvis Solaris = Earth + Air

However, the Egyptian and Jewish position was that:

Liquor Hepatis = Water + Air
Pulvis Solaris = Earth + Fire

Why is this distinction important? Because it refers to a vital part of the instructions given in the Emerald Tablet: *Separate the Earth from the Fire, the Subtle from the Gross, repeatedly with great skillfulness.* This formula refers to a specific step in the Experiment, in which each one of the second pair of compounds is reduced to its basic constituents.

The Earth element is separated from the Fire element in Pulvis Solaris; the Air (Subtle) element is separated from the Water (Gross) element in Liquor Hepatis. Water was considered grosser than Air, because in many ways, both physically and spiritually, Water symbolized the denser characteristics of Air.

Obviously, if we accept the interpretation of the Greek alchemists, the wording of rubric 2 makes no sense. Instead of saying "Separate the Earth from the Fire, the Subtle from the Gross," it would have to read, "Separate the Fire from the Gross, the Subtle from the Earth." This not only has no chemical basis, but it actually contradicts the thinking of Plato and Aristotle.

Why did the Alexandrian Greeks go against their own philosophical heritage and insist on such a pathological formulation of the Arcanum Experiment? Could their perversion have been a mere ruse to test the experimenter, to keep the Arcanum out of the hands of the unenlightened? This was certainly a major concern of the Greek alchemists.

The second rubric continues: *It rises from Earth to Heaven, and falls back again to Earth....* There can be no doubt that Liquor Hepatis has the ascending, superior role here, nor any doubt that Pulvis Solaris is the descending, inferior agent. This could be what confused the Greeks. They interpreted the Experiment to mean that Liquor Hepatis was made up of the superior elements Fire and Water. These were considered superior, because Fire contained Air, and Water contained Earth.

However, because of the circulatory nature of this part of the Experiment, the Liquor could as easily represent the Water and Air elements. The idea that both Water and Air can be superior is witnessed by the billowy clouds floating in the firmament. And do not the sun and stars exemplify the Fire and Earth burning in the heavens?

The circulatory pattern described here is confirmed by the ending lines of rubric 2: *...thereby containing within itself the powers of both the Above and the Below.* This refers to the pairs of superior and inferior elements separated out in the previous section; namely, the superior Fire and Water elements and the inferior Air and Earth elements of the two interacting compounds. By their exchange of elements, Pulvis Solaris and Liquor Hepatis each contain the powers of all Four Elements, the powers of Above and Below, when mixed in a solution of Vitriol and Natron.

In addition, the action of the Experiment in the second rubric is in accord with the action of the Experiment in the first rubric: *What is Below is like that which is Above. And that which is Above, like that which is Below, serve to bring the wonder of the Universe (or Experiment) into existence.* The first rubric introduces the first pair of compounds (Vitriol and Natron) used in the Arcanum Experiment, and the second rubric introduces the second pair of compounds Pulvis Solaris and Liquor Hepatis used in the Experiment.

The third rubric brings the compounds together as the Four Elements of the Four Arcana. This rubric states: *Thus will you obtain the glory of the entire Universe* (or Experiment). The glory of the entire universe is obtained by understanding the operation of the Four Elements at all levels of existence: in this Experiment, in nature, in stars, in the body, in the mind, and in the spirit.

Rubric 3 continues: *Every darkness will leave you.* This refers to knowledge beyond nature, to knowledge of the One. It is accomplished by achieving not only the Four Parts of this World, but also the single Arcanum, the Quintessence of the Experiment, which rules over the One World. In the Jewish interpretation of the Tabula, the concluding part of this rubric has its meaning in the Bible, however the Greek and the Egyptian interpretations treat it as simply an expression of perfect knowledge.

The actions of Liquor Hepatis and Pulvis Solaris are described in the Tabula in rubric 2: *Separate the Earth from the Fire....* This is the beginning of the Arcanum Experiment, where the mixing of the two compounds produces a moist steam. The Earth (Liquor Hepatis) is separated from the Fire (Pulvis Solaris) in the form of warm moisture. When the steaming has stopped, the result is a mixture of sulphuric acid and sodium salts. The salts settle to the bottom and the acid rises to the top. This is what is referred to in the first rubric: *And that which is Above is like that which is Below....*

The appearance of the elements in the Experiment is Earth/Fire, Water, Air, Earth. Because the Earth element (Liquor Hepatis) and the Fire element (Pulvis Solaris) react to make steam, together they represent water. So the order is actually: Water, Air, Earth. But the order presented in the *Tabula* is: Air, Earth, Water. The sequence described in the *Tabula* is not the actual order of events that take place in the Experiment, but instead reflects the order of events as described in Genesis. This was a major concession to the Jewish faction.

In this new light, we are able to grasp the meaning of the first rubric: *And that which is Above, like that which is Below, serve to bring the wonder of the universe into existence.* This obviously implies that the experiment is at an end. The mixing of Liquor Hepatis and Pulvis Solaris produces an active moisture, which eventually breaks down into sulphuric acid and Natron. The Natron settles to the bottom of the mixture as a crystalline salt and the acid goes to the top.

Rubric 2 describes the beginning of the experiment. We have identified the Pulvis Solaris mentioned in this revision as the Red Pulvis Solaris. It is formed by heating a mixture of mercury in nitric acid. The result is an impressive red steam and a red precipitate, which is used to make the Red Pulvis Solaris. This is an ascending/descending reaction.

We know that the ancient alchemists produced Liquor Hepatis by distilling of a mixture of sulphur, sal ammoniac, and lime. The reaction produces a combination of hydrogen sulfide and ammonia gases. What is left behind is a reddish brown Liquor. Since nothing settles out, this is only an ascending reaction—a significant fact considering this arcanum is associated with the soul.

When Pulvis Solaris and Liquor Hepatis are mixed together, the powder sinks to the bottom and produces a distinctive red steam. In all the reactions involving Pulvis Solaris and Liquor Hepatis, the things that ascend are ammonia, hydrogen sulfide, and the red steam. What descends are always red precipitates.

So let us follow the *Tabula* in terms of this Experiment: The red vapor and the red precipitate rise from the bottom to the top of the container, and the red precipitate falls back down again to the bottom, thereby containing within itself the powers of both the Above and the Below. That means that the vapor generated by the experiment ascends, and is composed of the vapor generated by the upper Liquor Hepatis and the bubbles of gas released by the lower Pulvis Solaris. The gas bubbles attached to the Pulvis Solaris cause pieces to move up in the reaction and then fall back down as the bubbles are broken. A mixture of three gases is generated: ammonia, hydrogen sulfide, and red-stained water vapor.

Separate the Earth from the Fire, the Subtle from the Gross, repeatedly with great skillfulness discusses the formation of Liquor Hepatis through repeated distillations of the solution of sulphur, sal ammoniac, and lime. In this reaction, it was clear to the alchemists that Fire was represented by the sulphur in the hydrogen sulphide gas, and Earth was represented by the sulphur in its solid state. Therefore sulphur is made up of both Fire and Earth, and it embodies the relationship between Fire and Earth.

The Subtle is ammonia as a liquid and a gas. It is subtle because it represents the fertility in matter. The Gross is the red moisture as vapor and as common water. It was Gross to Jewish alchemists because water is the matrix of creation in the world according to the Bible. The Subtle ammonia and Fire part of sulphur remain above as the Liquor. The Gross water and the Earth part of sulphur go under as precipitates.

So the first part of rubric 2 means: Above is subtle ammonia (as gas), sulphur as Fire and Earth (in hydrogen sulfide gas and as solid sulphur), and gross Water (as red vapor). Now separate sulphur as Earth from sulphur as Fire. Also separate subtle ammonia from gross Water. These operations are accomplished with many repeated distillations, which purifies the elements for the perfection of the Experiment.

The First Chapter of Genesis begins: *In the beginning God created the heavens and the earth. Then the earth was formless and empty, darkness was over the surface of the deep, and the Spirit of God was hovering over the waters.* The order of creation was heaven, earth, and water.

In this light, it is possible to understand the meaning of the next verse in rubric 2: *It rises from Earth to Heaven, and falls back again to Earth,....* The passage describes how Pulvis Solaris rises up, as does the Liquor Hepatis. The difference is that the Liquor remains above, while the Pulvis Solaris descends again. On a microcosmic scale, the Arcanum Experiment symbolized the Great Experiment of God, the Universe itself.

The remainder of rubric 2 says: *...thereby containing within itself the powers of the Above and the Below.* This is concerned with the Liquor, Pulvis, and entire moisture from the standpoint of their original separation and creation.

The third rubric underscores the fact that the Arcanum Experiment parallels the Story of Genesis: *Thus will you obtain the glory of the entire Universe.* In fact, it seems to imply that some further reflection is required before "Every darkness will leave you."

In the previous section we discovered four of the seven arcana of alchemy. During the course of the Experiment three hidden (or higher) arcana are formed by the actions of the experimenter on the original compounds, just as the actions of God created three hidden principles in the world. We do not know what the Alexandrians called these three hidden principles, but later alchemists called them Mercury, sulphur, and Salt. If philosophical Mercury and sulphur were formed in the preparation of the Pulvis Solaris, philosophical Salt will precipitate in the course of the Experiment. These subtle (or divine) elements are necessary for the successful completion of the Experiment.

So in the First Revision, we have four chemical arcana and three philosophical arcana, or seven arcana altogether. In the Jewish interpretation there must be seven arcana, because in their numerology, seven is the number of perfection.

By the fourth rubric we have obtained all seven arcana, at least in the Jewish sense. We have "the greatest strength (or vitality) of all." The completed Arcanum "...conquers every subtle thing and penetrates every solid thing." This of course includes the human body and suggests that the Arcanum can be used as a healing agent.

A justification for the Jewish compromise position can be found in the Old Testament. The author considers the Nineteenth Psalm to be a biblical parallel to the Emerald Tablet:

1. A Psalm of David for all to sing.
2. The heavens declare the glory of God; the skies show his handy work.
3. Day after day they utter speech, and night after night they display their knowledge.
4. But they have no speech, there are no words; no sound is heard from them.
5. Yet their voice is gone out through all the earth, their words to the end of the world. In them has he set a tabernacle for the sun.

6. He is like a bridegroom coming out of his chamber, like a champion rejoicing to run his course.
7. His going forth is from one end of heaven to the other; nothing is hidden from his heat.
8. The law of the Lord is complete and quickens the soul. The statutes of the Lord are trustworthy, making wise the simple.
9. The commands of the Lord are right, rejoicing the heart. The precepts of the Lord are pure, giving light to the eyes.
10. The fear of the Lord is spotless, enduring forever. The judgments of the Lord are sure and altogether righteous.
11. More to be desired are they than gold, than much pure gold; sweeter are they than honey, than honey from the comb.
12. Moreover, by them is your servant warned, and in keeping with them there is great reward.
13. Who can discern his own errors? Cleanse me from hidden faults.
14. Keep back your servant from presumptuous sins; let them not rule over me. Then shall I be upright and innocent of the great transgression.
15. Let the words of my mouth and the meditation of my heart be acceptable in your sight, O Lord, my Rock and my Redeemer.

The first seven verses of this Psalm deal with Jewish cosmology. Early scholars named this Psalm *Gloria Dei* from the phrase "glory of God" in the second verse. The term *Gloria Dei* also refers to the goal of alchemy and was used to describe the art for many centuries. The alchemical undertones become clear by verses 8 and 9. The law of God, the statutes of God, the command of God, and the precepts of God mentioned in these verses are synonyms for the four Arcana: Liquor Hepatis, Pulvis Solaris, Vitriol, and Natron. The fear of God and the judgments of God mentioned in verse 10 describe the way the arcana are attracted to one another: Liquor Hepatis for Pulvis Solaris, and Vitriol for Natron. Thus, Verse 11 alludes to the power of the arcana over metals, as well as the mineral and vegetative kingdoms.

Verse 12 speaks directly to the alchemist and hints at the miracles available to him. Verse 13 admonishes the alchemist that progress cannot be made unless he is himself pure. Verse 14 warns of the curse of hubris, the blinding pride that befalls all who seek to understand nature. It cautions that the forces of alchemy not only rule over all material interactions, but can also overcome the alchemist himself.

The Egyptian interpretation of the alchemical work offers a different emphasis. The central symbol of Egyptian alchemy was the Nile River. It separated their desert landscape into heaven and earth. Heaven was further divided into the blue sky and the starry cosmos, but earth, for the Egyptians, was Egypt. Of course, they were aware of the rest of the world, but what went on in the rest of the world was of little concern to them. They felt favored by

God, and God's greatest gift was the Nile. The Nile flowed only through Egypt. Without the Nile, there was no Egypt.

The Nile rose and fell by mysterious forces. Sometimes it overflowed its banks, and all that could be seen was water and sky. On the horizon, where the water ended and heaven began, the river merged with the sky. When it finally returned to its river bed, the Nile brought back with it a bit of heaven.

So whenever the Egyptian alchemists spoke of earth, they meant Egypt with the Nile. Whenever they spoke of heaven, they meant the firmament of the sky with the sun, moon, and stars. The Nile mediated between all of them and embodied what later alchemists came to call the Mercurial Principle.

In the *Tabula*, the Egyptians interpreted "what is Above" to mean Heaven and "what is Below" to mean the created world. Earth to them was Egypt, and Fire represented the sun, moon, and stars. The subtle element was Air, as contained in the firmament. The gross element was Water, as in the Greek Jewish interpretations, except it sometimes referred specifically to the waters of the Nile.

It is with the second rubric that the Egyptian interpretation differs in significant ways from that of the Jews and Greeks. The first part of this rubric says: *Separate the Earth from the Fire, the Subtle from the Gross....* To that the Egyptians would have added: *Separate the Earth from the Gross, the Subtle from the Fire*, which would have meant to separate the Nile from Egypt, the firmament from the sun, moon, and stars.

In other words, the phrase "separate...repeatedly with great skillfulness" meant much more than simply to isolate the superior and inferior elements. It meant to further differentiate heaven into the firmament (or sky) and the cosmos (sun, moon, and stars). It meant to split earth into Egypt and the Nile. This supports the assertion that the Egyptians had learned to break down the four compounds of the Arcanum Experiment into their constituent elements.

The second rubric continues: *It rises from Earth to Heaven, and falls back again to Earth, thereby containing within itself the powers of both the Above and the Below*. The Nile overflowed its banks and climbed up from Egypt to reach the firmament. There it took heaven to its bed, and brought back a sacred fertility, when it returned to its shores. Thus the Nile received the powers of the Above and the Below. It merged Egypt with the firmament, and the sun, the moon, and the stars.

The third rubric: *Thus will you obtain the glory of the entire Universe...* suggests that Egypt is the highest expression of both the Above and the Below, but only as far as it remains identified with the Nile. The fourth rubric speaks again of the Nile, positioning it as ruler of all elements in both heaven and earth: *This is the greatest strength of all, because it conquers every subtle thing and penetrates every solid thing.*

The foregoing Egyptian cosmology formed the basis of their alchemy. The concealed chemical reactions in the Emerald Tablet were every bit as obvious to the high priests of Egypt as they were to the more empirical Greeks. These chemical principles were considered too powerful to be divulged to the uninitiated masses, and for that reason, the Egyptian faction sought to prevent their full disclosure in the Tabula. Instead, the priests sought to increase their influence over the populace by accentuating a spiritual interpretation. This spiritual motif proceeded by interpreting the rubrics in the following manner:

Rubric 1: Our soul originates from God in heaven and our body originates from earth. Thus the superior in man or animals is the soul, and the inferior is the body. The soul combined with the body is the living body that brings about all creation in the world.

Rubric 2: The Earth separated from the Fire and the Gross separated from the Subtle create the superior and inferior components of humans and animals. The superior is further separated into Fire and the Subtle, representing the human soul and the animal soul. The inferior is further separated into Earth and the Gross, representing the human body and the animal body.
(The repeated separations referred to in this rubric represent the Egyptian idea of reincarnation. At death, the superior part (soul) returns to heaven and the inferior part (body) returns to earth. The soul then returns to earth in a new body, which can be either human or animal.)

Rubric 3: The reincarnation of the soul into different bodies is the glorification of the universe, an evolutionary process which perfects the soul.

Rubric 4: This describes the perfected soul as the greatest strength of all, because it conquers every subtle thing and penetrates every solid thing. It is something at home both in heaven and on earth.

Chapter Four

The Second Revision: The *Tabula Hermetica*

The author of the Second Revision was a Jew of the First Alexandrian Period. His revision of the Tabula was written around 270 B.C. and came to be called the *Tabula Hermetica*. Although the Jewish story of Genesis had been incorporated into the First Revision, the numerology embedded within the document was of Greek origin. The author of the Second Revision set out to remedy that situation.

In the First Revision, the number Two is represented as the dichotomy of the superior and inferior elements. The number Four is represented as the four arcana (Vitriol, Natron, Pulvis Solaris, and Liquor Hepatis), which can also be represented by the number Three. As we have seen, this is because Liquor Hepatis and Pulvis Solaris can be considered as one element (Air or moist vapor). The number One is represented in the third verse as the "One Thing."

Thus the numerology is 1,2,3,4. These are the numbers through which the Greeks ordered the elements and the natural world.

On the other hand, Jewish numerology focused on the first seven integers, based on the seven days of creation in Genesis. Of these, the numbers Three and Seven were considered esoteric (having secret or divine meanings), while the other numbers were considered exoteric (for the public). As Jewish influence in Alexandria grew, Jewish alchemists more vigorously protested the Greek numerology of the First Revision.

Since the First Revision had already achieved some authority among alchemists, a substantial revision was not possible. The last sentence in the previous revision (*What I have said concerning the operation of the Sun is complete*) was omitted in the Second Revision. Other than this, not a single new word was added or subtracted; only the arrangement and punctuation of the rubrics was changed. Nonetheless, changes in the punctuation of the second rubric did require that the verb "serve" be referenced twice instead of just once as in the First Revision. In that same rubric, the word "wonder" was pluralized. These minor alterations allowed major differences in interpretation between the First and Second Revisions.

Rubric 1: It is true without lie, certain and most true.

Rubric 2: What is Below, serves, like that which is Above, and that which is Above, serves, like that which is Below, to bring the wonders of the Universe into existence. And as all things originate from One Thing, from the Idea of One Mind: so do all created things originate from this One Thing through adaptation.

Rubric 3: Its father is the Sun, its mother the Moon. The Wind carries it in its belly, its nurse is the Earth. It is the father of all existing things in the entire Universe, its inherent virtue is perfected when it is changed into Earth. Separate the Earth from the Fire, the Subtle from the Gross, repeatedly with great skillfulness. It rises from Earth to Heaven, and falls back down again to Earth, thereby containing within itself the powers of the Above and the Below.

Rubric 4: Thus will you obtain the glory of the entire Universe. Every darkness will leave you.

Rubric 5: This is the greatest strength of all, because it conquers every subtle thing and penetrates every "solid thing."

Rubric 6: In this way, was the Universe created. From this proceeds wonders, of which herewith is an example.

Rubric 7: Therefore, I am called the three-times glorified Hermes, because I possess all three parts of the true understanding of the whole Universe.

Within the *Tabula* there exists an indirect numerology and a direct numerology. The indirect numerology arises out of the basic premise of the Tabula, namely, "As Above, so Below." For instance, the *Tabula* states that all things are created from One Thing. Therefore there must be One Arcanum able to create or transmute matter. Also, since the world is made up of four directions and four aspects of creation (the blue sky, the heavenly bodies, the land, and the sea), this One Arcanum must consist of the four major arcana. These concepts are implied in the Second Revision.

The direct numerology in the Second Revision can be interpreted in the following manner:

Rubric 1: The number Two is presented first. The word "true" is repeated at the beginning and end of this sentence and represents the number Two. In addition the major arcana can be divided into two groups of opposing qualities: solid or liquid, rising or falling, etc. For example, iron and Pulvis Solaris are solids, while sulphuric acid and Liquor Hepatis are liquids. The number Two (as duality, separation, and dialogue) symbolizes the recognition of truth. It symbolizes the empirical facts of the material world and the knowledge of opposites.

Rubric 2: This rubric is associated with the number Five. These are the five phases of creation according to Genesis. They are the previously existing Logos and the Fire (or adaptation) of the first day of creation, the Air and Water of the second day, and the Earth of the third day. The number five is also implied in the material separation of each of the major arcana. Natron becomes sodium carbonate and sodium nitrate. This gives us five arcanum: these two sodium compounds plus the three remaining arcana (Vitriol, Pulvis Solaris, and Liquor Hepatis). If one separates Pulvis Solaris into the Red and the Black powders, the addition of the other arcana (Natron, Vitriol, and Liquor Hepatis) also gives the number five. If Vitriol is separated into sulphuric acid and iron, then the addition of the remaining three arcana (Pulvis Solaris, Natron, and Liquor Hepatis) gives five again. Significantly, only three of the four major arcana were separated. The early alchemists would not separate Liquor Hepatis, because they associated it with the soul. The number five symbolized the Quintessence, the union of matter (the two material aspects of each arcana) with the divine (the three remaining unseparated arcana).

Rubric 3: The esoteric number Three is represented here as the three Jewish arcana with which this rubric deals. The Jewish alchemists recognized only the three elements of Genesis (Water, Air, and Earth). For them, the Air element was a combination of Liquor Hepatis and Pulvis Solaris, because mixing them produced a red vapor. The number Three stands for synthesis and solution.

Rubric 4: The esoteric number Seven is represented by this rubric. The "glory of the entire Universe" is obtained through the three arcana of Jewish alchemy. However, "every darkness will leave you" only by completing the first four arcana. Together they total the seven arcana: sulphuric Acid, Iron, Sodium Carbonate, Sodium Nitrate, Red Pulvis Solaris, Black Pulvis Solaris, and Liquor Hepatis. Seven is a symbol of perfection and mystical union.

Rubric 5: The representation of the number Four here is the same as in the First Revision. It stands for the four powers of the arcana, as well as the four major arcana themselves: Vitriol, Natron, Pulvis Solaris, and Liquor Hepatis. Four represents the orderly arrangement of what has been separated in nature.

Rubric 6: The number One is signified here. The miracle of all alchemical knowledge unified into one text is offered in the Emerald Tablet. Moreover, the wonders of the One Arcanum made by the unification of the four major arcana are promised. This is the Elixir or Stone of alchemy. The number One is associated with light and union with God.

Rubric 7: The final rubric represents the number Six. The number three is repeated twice, alluding to the two overlapping triangles of the Star of David, which also represents the union of fire and water in the human soul. Furthermore, a grouping of the arcana into six is accomplished by separating two of the major arcana into their constituent compounds. For example, dividing Natron and Pulvis Solaris into their parts gives the following six arcana: Sodium Carbonate, Sodium Nitrate, Red Pulvis, Black Pulvis, Vitriol, and Liquor Hepatis. Or separating Vitriol and Pulvis Solaris into their respective halves: sulphuric acid, Iron, Red Pulvis, Black Pulvis, Natron, and Liquor Hepatis. In a like manner, the splitting of Natron and Vitriol will give a third group of six arcana.

As to the Jewish interpretation of the Second Revision, the first rubric is the introduction. It assures us that the *Tabula* is a most serious and a most true document.

The second rubric is the Cosmological Rubric, which presents the story of creation from the Bible. The effect of the punctuation changes here is to separate the Above and the Below into two distinct pairs of superior and inferior elements. The three elements of Genesis are present as the Above (Water and Air) and the Below (Earth). Again, Water is placed above, because it is thought to contain Earth based on the Water Transformation Experiment. So we have two superior/inferior pairs: Water and Earth; Air and Earth.

This differentiation into two distinct pairs is underscored by reversing the order of the key words at the beginning of this rubric: What is Below, serves, like that which is Above, and that which is Above, serves, like that which is Below, to bring the wonders of the Universe into existence. By referring to "wonders" as plural, the author further implies that more than one group of superior and inferior elements are intended.

This rubric continues: *And as all things originate from One Thing, from the Idea of One Mind: so do all created things originate from this One Thing through adaptation.* The "One Thing" from the Jewish standpoint is not the *Materia Prima* of the Greeks, but a paternal God symbolizing the primal forces present at the beginning of Genesis. The logos is present as "the Idea of One Mind."

The term "all created things" refers to the first day of the created world, where Air, Water, and Earth are expressed as sky, sea, and land. The key word in this rubric is adaptation, for it is through creative action (Fire) that the sun, moon, and stars are accounted for on this first full day of creation. *Let there be Light*, God said.

The crucial third rubric, the only one whose position matches its esoteric number, describes the Arcanum Experiment itself. This is the Arcanum Rubric. Sulphuric acid and Natron are present in the occult Water, and by the action of Fire we create Liquor Hepatis and Pulvis Solaris—*Its father is the Sun, its mother the Moon. The Wind carries it in its belly, its nurse is the Earth. It is the father of all existing things in the entire Universe. Its inherent virtue is perfected when it is changed into Earth.* The pronoun "it" refers to the Water of creation for the Jewish alchemist or to the First Matter for the Greeks. In the Arcanum Experiment, the occult Water consists of two things: Sulphuric acid and Natron.

The first three verses of this rubric are each separated into two clauses by a comma. The first part of each of these sentences refers to sulphuric acid, the second part refers to Natron. The first part of rubric 3 then reads: *Sulphuric acid is the active Sun or father, Natron is the passive Moon or mother. Sulphuric acid carries the Wind in its belly (vapor forms above it), Natron is nursed by the earth (mined from it). The nature of sulphuric acid (action) is the father of all existing things in the Universe, the virtue of Natron (salt) is perfected when it grows within the Earth.*

Paralleling the structure of the second rubric, we now introduce the notion of Fire. As we have stated earlier, Liquor Hepatis is composed of Air, Water, and Fire; Pulvis Solaris is composed of Air, Earth, and Fire. Thus the elements which differentiate them are Water in the Liquor Hepatis and Earth in the Pulvis Solaris. They share the elements Air and Fire.

The last two verses in rubric 3 refer to the application of Fire (heating) to the mixture of all four arcana. *Separate the Earth from the Fire, the Subtle from the Gross, repeatedly with great skillfulness. It rises from Earth to Heaven, and falls back down again to Earth, thereby containing within itself the powers of the Above and the Below.* The currents of the heated mixture agitate the elements and a white fog (ammonia) forms over the acid. Further heating causes water vapor (red steam) to form. Next the precipitate is lifted above by the action of the currents and the red gas bubbles which have attached to its surface. When it reaches the surface, the precipitate submerges again to the bottom of the solution. This circulation is repeated many times.

Therefore by application of Fire to the mixture of compounds in the occult Water, Liquor Hepatis and Pulvis Solaris are broken up into their constituent elements of Air (gas), Water (steam), Earth (precipitate) and Fire (hot gases, steam, and solids). The second part of rubric 3 now reads:

Separate the Earth from the Fire in Pulvis Solaris, separate the Air from the Water in Liquor Hepatis, repeatedly with great skillfulness. The precipitated matter rises from the Bottom to the Top of its container, and falls back down to the Bottom, thereby incorporating the forces at the Top and Bottom of the experiment.

The fourth rubric is the *Gloria* Rubric. It implies that once the Arcanum of the previous rubric is achieved, the alchemist has obtained "the glory of the whole universe." We have noted that the numerology of the *Tabula* was altered, so that it no longer reflected a linear progression (1, 2, 3, 4, 5, 6) to the final goal of perfection (7). Rather the numbers were divided into exoteric (1, 2, 4, 5, 6) and esoteric (3, 7) sets.

This change reflects a fundamental revelation of Jewish alchemy. To them, the success of the Experiment depended not only on an orderly adherence to specified (exoteric) steps, but also required the application of secret (esoteric) methods. Thus the Experiment has both rational (material) and irrational (divine) components. Only in this way will—*Every darkness leave you.* Divine assistance is required.

The fifth rubric is the Elixir Rubric. It describes the medicinal properties of the Arcanum: *It is the greatest strength of all, because it conquers every subtle thing and penetrates every solid thing.* In the Latin and Greek versions, the word "strength" appears after the third word "greatest." From the standpoint of the preceding *Gloria* Rubric, this implies that three of the seven arcana may be valuable in healing and prolonging life. This also reflects the dogma of the First Alexandrian School, which stated that the world was composed of three elements: Solid, Liquid, and Gas. Therefore the Elixir must work on the three elements in the human body: solid flesh and bone, liquid blood and lymph, gases and breath.

The sixth rubric is the Index. "In this way, was the Universe created" refers back to the first part of rubric 2, the Cosmological Rubric. That section recapitulates the story of creation in which God "created Heaven and Earth," thereby causing the primal separation of the Above and the Below. *From this proceeds wonders...* refers back to the second part of this rubric, which states that all things originate from One Thing through adaptation. The disclosure of the three healing arcana within the words of the Tabula is alluded to by the phrase "...herewith is an example." The seventh rubric is the Conclusion: *Therefore, I am called the three-times glorified Hermes, because I possess all three parts of the true understanding of the whole Universe.* The name here is that of Hermes Trismegistus. Mythologically, he has been associated with the Egyptian god Thoth, the Greek god Hermes, and the Roman god Mercury. As a god, he certainly became three-times glorified. As the guide to both the Above and the Below, the companion of all those dead to the world, he became the patron-spirit of alchemy. Beyond this, we find final confirmation that the number of the arcana is three. We find the secret buried in rubric three, in the three arcane substances alluded to there.

The Greek alchemists had little objection to the changes proposed by the Jewish faction. First of all, they felt that they had incorporated their ideas into the First Revision, and realized major modifications were no longer possible. In fact, some of them must have felt they had been too obvious. Although non-alchemists were totally bewildered by the meaning of the four rubrics, why not add to their frustration by rearranging the *Tabula* into seven rubrics?

Since the Greeks believed the number Four was the key to the Arcanum, they had no problem concealing it deeper within the structure of the *Tabula*. The Pythagorean philosophy of numbers allowed them to interpret the remaining numbers in a traditional Greek fashion, which saw numbers as a kind of *Materia Prima* of the universe. During this period, many Greek philosophers were preoccupied with trying to understand the relationship between the One and the Many.

Again, the first rubric is seen as an introduction. It sets the entire tone of the work.

The second rubric is the Elements Rubric. As we have seen, the changes in this rubric make it clear that it now refers to two distinct pairs of Above and Below elements. For the Greeks, these were Water and Earth on the one hand, and Fire and Air on the other. The second part of this rubric, "...all things originate from One Thing, from the idea of One Mind...," did not refer to any god. Rather it described an idealization of the number One, before the division into duality. The primal unity was visualized as a chaotic, all-encompassing First Matter. The idea, or meditation, of One Mind was the universal Logos, the shaping force behind this *Materia Prima*.

In the Pythagorean sense, the number One was not a real number. It was beyond comprehension, like the dimensionless single point it symbolized. However, the number One was a necessary beginning for the whole succession of numbers, and for that matter, all of physical reality. The rubric continues: *...so do all things originate from this One Thing through adaptation.*

The original Latin uses the word *adoptione*, which could be translated as adoption, instead of adaptation. This would restore more of the Greek sense to this rubric, for Pythagoras thought of Unity as the father of all numbers. By adopting each number one at a time, Unity generated the series of whole numbers; by adopting a zero, Unity became 10. In this way, all the Pythagorean numbers could be considered present within the *Tabula*.

The Greeks saw the third rubric as the Cosmological/Arcanological Rubric. "Its father is the Sun, its mother the moon" described the shining canopy of heavenly bodies. "The Wind carried it in its belly" refers to the fact that Air is the mother of the firmament (atmosphere), while its nurse is the Earth suggests that the Earth helps create the atmosphere that envelopes it. Therefore, the first part of this rubric presents the formation of the heavens from an empirical standpoint.

As regards the arcana, Liquor Hepatis consists of the elements Water and Air. It represented by the firmament (air) with clouds (water vapor). Pulvis Solaris consists of the elements Earth and Fire, and is represented by the fiery sun and stars with the solid planets and moon.

The third rubric continues: *It is the father of all existing things in the entire Universe.* To the Greeks, this meant three separate worlds: the cosmos, the ideal world, and the elemental world. As we have learned the elements were arranged in a hierarchy: Water, Earth, Fire, Air. The first, was Water, which they considered the head (father) of the family. Water was perfected when turned into the primordial water. This primordial water was Vitriol, which was considered the chemical father of the other arcana. The Earth arcanum was represented by the salts of Natron. The Fire arcanum was Pulvis Solaris, and the Air arcanum was Liquor Hepatis. The rest of this rubric concerns arcana as they react in the Arcanum Experiment, and the Greek interpretation was necessarily the same as the Jewish interpretation described above.

The fourth rubric was also the *Gloria* Rubric for the Greeks, announcing the miracles of the Arcanum—"Thus will you obtain the glory of the entire Universe. Every darkness will leave you."

The "greatest strength of all" in the fifth rubric refers to the four arcana of the Greeks: Vitriol, Natron, Liquor Hepatis, and Pulvis Solaris. This is the Elixir rubric and the Greeks believed that it required four, not three, ingredients.

The sixth rubric is the Index. Again, this rubric refers back to the second rubric, the Elements Rubric. "In this way, was the Universe created..." talks about the four elements of the Greek empiricist view of creation.

The concluding seventh rubric states: *Therefore, I am called the three-times glorified Hermes, because I possess all three parts of the true understanding of the whole Universe.* From the Greek standpoint, this rubric confirms that the *Tabula* is a combination of all three philosophies of the world (the Egyptian, the Greek, and the Jewish). The title for the *Tabula* preferred by the Greeks would have been simply:—The Combined Philosophy of the Whole World.

Two verses in the *Tabula* suggest a strong Egyptian influence. "Its father is the Sun and its mother the Moon, ...its nurse is the Earth" is strict Egyptian cosmology. In ancient hieroglyphics, the Egyptians called themselves the "sons of the Sun." One inscription at Memphis calls Ptolemy the son of the Sun, and there are many similar references to pharaohs and scholars of the time. Another inscription at Luxor calls Egypt "the nurse" of the Sun's power.

The other Egyptian verse is the final rubric, which deals with the Egyptian god, Thoth. Hermes was the name given by the Greeks to this ancient Egyptian god of wisdom. He was considered the scribe of the gods and all sacred texts were attributed to him. By putting this rubric at the end of the *Tabula*, all parties are recognizing the Egyptian source of the original work.

Thoth was also the guide of souls after death or separation from the body. He showed them the way to heaven. By assimilating Thoth as Hermes, the Greeks paid a gesture of great homage to the ancient Egyptians, much as the Romans did when they accepted Hermes as their own god Mercury.

Furthermore, because Thoth was the guide of the dead, there is some support for the idea that the original *Tabula* served as a tombstone, as many of the legends surrounding Hermes suggest. If the *Tabula Smaragdina* was intended as a monument at the grave of Hermes, then that explains why the *Tabula* was inscribed on a tablet of green stone and not on reed cloth or parchment.

As with the First Revision, the official Egyptian interpretation of the Second Revision was spiritual. Only the highest circle of priests knew of the Arcanum Experiment, knowledge of which was transmitted by word of mouth. The Egyptians would never disseminate such knowledge to the uninitiated.

In the Second Revision the Egyptian priests saw the opportunity to elaborate their descriptions of the god Thoth. Three times glorified described the trinity of souls represented by the one god Thoth. Thoth was not only the One Soul, but also could be represented as a having three souls. These were the Fire Soul, the Air Soul, and the Earth Soul.

The Fire Soul manifested itself in the process of metabolism in man and animals. The slow burning of food in the body and its transformation into excrement confirmed the description of Fire as the agent of transformation. When the body died, the Fire Soul remained in the body causing decay and putrefaction.

The Air Soul was seen as the breathing process in men and animals. The Egyptians associated the presence of a soul with breath, because a living body breathed regularly and a dead body did not. The Air Soul left the body at death.

The Earth Soul was part of man's close ties to the planet itself. It nourished him and protected him. Man's own body was of the earth and was returned to it when he died.

From the Egyptian standpoint, the first part of the Tabula (from *It is true without lie...* to *...Its inherent virtue is perfected when it is changed into Earth*) described the properties of these three souls.

The souls of animals were inferior (what is Below) to the souls of men (what is Above), but all souls served to bring the wonders of the One Soul into existence. From this One Soul emanated all the created Universe (through adaptation). The Fire Soul is the source of all souls, since the Sun and Moon are the fiery parents which give them birth. The Air Soul carries these souls in its belly, and the Earth Soul is their nurse. The One Soul is the father of all existing things in the entire Universe.

Continuing from rubric 3 through rubric 5 (from *Separate the Earth from the Fire...* to *...penetrates every solid thing*), the subject now includes material bodies. If we separate the Fire Soul (Fire) from its body (Earth, matter) and the Air Soul (the Subtle) from its body (the Gross, living body), then we reunite the lower souls with the higher One Soul. This is what happens when we die. The soul rises from earth to heaven, where it is weighed (or judged) and falls back down again to earth (is reincarnated), thereby containing within itself the powers of the Above and the Below. Thus the greatest strength of all is the immortal soul, which conquers (survives) every subtle thing (the cycle of life and death) and penetrates every solid thing (every incarnated body).

The two sentences of rubric 6 (*In this way was the Universe created. From this proceeds wonders.*) refer back to the second rubric, which discusses the emanation of all souls from the One Soul. The trinity of souls that make up the One Soul above is reflected in the trinity of souls that make up the our own (Many) souls below.

Rubric 7 associates Hermes with Thoth. It also indicates that the Egyptian interpretation of the Emerald Tablet is made up of the three sections described above; that is, all three parts of the true understanding of the whole Universe. So altogether, the Egyptian interpretation of the Second Revision contains a total of four sections, that could have been rewritten into just four rubrics.

Now we come to a most astonishing feature of numerology of the Egyptian version of the Second Revision. Each of the four sections consists of two subsections expressing different ideas. The first section presents the One Soul above and the many souls below. The second section describes the soul in death and rebirth. The third section again refers to the trinity of souls both above and below. The fourth section not only presents Thoth as Hermes, but suggests that the three preceding sections are the true philosophy of the Universe.

Therefore, the four main sections of the Egyptian rendering consist of eight indirect rubrics. In Egyptian numerology, four is the number of the created world and eight is the number of Thoth. Throughout their religion, they associated the number eight with this god of wisdom. In fact, the Egyptian name of the holy city of Hermopolis (which was in Middle Egypt) is Shmun, which means Eight. Even the final version of the Second Revision, which consists of seven rubrics, would have consisted of eight had the final rubric not been omitted. We will find in the later interpretations of the Tabula, that the numerology once again returns to the number eight.

Chapter Five

The Third Revision: *Tabula de Operatione Solis*

We cannot say with any certainty whether the author of the Third Revision was Greek, or Jewish, or some other nationality. All we know is that he was a cosmopolitan thinker, a citizen of the world. His revision appeared sometime between 50 B.C. and 1 A.D. It became known as the *Tabula de Operatione Solis*. The goal of the author was to expose the metaphysical principles in the *Tabula* that would allow men to make gold. He thus tried to broaden the scope of the *Tabula* while not altering its wording substantially, since it had become a revered canon of philosophy.

He started by redefining rubrics 3, 4, and 5. Then he changed the meaning of a word in the second rubric. The original Greek word for adaptation could also be translated as adoption. He chose the later translation. He also restored the last rubric from the First Revision, in what appeared a harmless addition. By doing so, he changed the numerology of the document from 7 to 8, but not necessarily to emphasize the Egyptian numerology. The restored rubric allowed an eighth arcana to be introduced.

His interpretation of the new revision became extremely popular. It would change the course of alchemy, giving it new impetus, yet at the same time planting the seed of alchemy's eventual demise. The metaphysical Interpretation contained principles that allowed fakirs and charlatans to dupe people into believing they knew how to change nearly anything into gold. The Third Revision of the Emerald Tablet is as follows:

Rubric 1: It is true without lie, certain and most true.

Rubric 2: What is Below, serves, like that which is Above, and that which is Above, serves, like that which is Below, to bring the wonders of the Universe into existence. And as all things originate from One Thing, from the Idea of One Mind: so do all created things originate from this One Thing through adoption.

Rubric 3: Its father is the Sun, its mother the Moon. The Wind carries it in its belly, its nurse is the Earth.

Rubric 4: It is the father of all existing things in the entire Universe, its inherent virtue is perfected when it is changed into Earth. Separate the Earth from the Fire, the Subtle from the Gross, repeatedly with great skillfulness. It rises from Earth to Heaven, and falls back down again to Earth, thereby containing within itself the powers of the Above and the Below.

Rubric 5: Thus will you obtain the glory of the entire Universe. Every darkness will leave you. This is the greatest strength of all, because it conquers every subtle thing and penetrates every solid thing.

Rubric 6: In this way, was the Universe created. From this proceeds wonders, of which herewith is an example.

Rubric 7: Therefore, I am called the three-times glorified Hermes, because I possess all three parts of the true understanding of the whole Universe.

Rubric 8: What I have had to say about the operation of the Sun is completed.

By restoring the final rubric, the *Tabula* took on a more subjective tone. The phrase "the operation of the Sun" was interpreted to mean just one thing: the art of making gold. Three centuries earlier this phrase meant the workings of God symbolized by the movement of the sun in the heavens. The Arcanum of the Sun was Red Pulvis Solaris (primarily red mercuric oxide). The author of the Third Revision took this to mean that red mercuric oxide was the actual material that could be changed into gold and that could, by itself, change other materials into gold.

The key to the process was rubric 5: *...it conquers every subtle thing and penetrates every solid thing.* To the alchemists at the time, this meant that the red mercuric oxide contained the metaphysical seed of transformation that would cause the red oxide, or other objects, to be changed into gold. In that sense it came to be called "the Red Mercury of Transformation."

From the First Century all the way to the Middle Ages, alchemists began identifying almost any red chemical, mineral, or metal as the Red Mercury of Transformation. A good example is red orpiment, which they also called Hydrargyrum ruber (red mercury). Orpiment is a mineral that contains neither mercury nor gold. It is a sulfide of arsenic that occurs in both red and yellow varieties. The alchemists mistakenly assumed that the red orpiment was slowly changing into gold and called it Red Mercury.

Pliny reported in *Historia Naturalis*: "There is an Art which allows one to make gold from orpiment. Orpiment is found buried not far under the earth in Syria, sometimes has a golden color, and is as brittle as glass. It forms the basis of a yellow paint called Royal Yellow." He went on to warn his readers that not all such efforts were successful. He cited the example of a certain prince, who had secured vast quantities of orpiment and told everyone he succeeded in making a small quantity of pure gold. But only the prince believed he had made real gold. When he showed his gold nuggets to anyone, all they saw were gold-painted stones.

Pliny's precautionary tale underscores the proliferation of the art of goldmaking during the first century A.D. Most of these efforts were inspired by the metaphysical view of the *Tabula*, in which non-physical correspondences were assumed responsible for the transformation of baser metals into gold. Swindlers, fools, and cheats used this line of thinking to justify using almost any red or yellow-colored substance to try to change base materials into gold. The name of alchemy became associated with the practice of making fake gold. The situation became so bad, that Roman rulers outlawed both the study of alchemy and the study of mathematics (with the exception of geometry), believing both to be black arts.

The first rubric is still the Introductory Rubric, however the phrase "certain and most true" was interpreted in the sense of "certain and most veritable." That is to say, we can directly experience the truths presented here.

In the second rubric, the Above or superior phenomena is the red vapor that floats above the mixture of mercury and nitric acid during the formation of red mercuric oxide. The Below or inferior phenomena is the red precipitate that falls to the bottom of that same solution. Both the red vapor and the red solid at the bottom are the same thing: red mercuric oxide. Since both the Above and the Below "serve to bring the wonders of the universe into existence," red mercuric oxide is the "One Thing" through which all created things originate.

Rubric 2 continues: *And as all things originate from One Thing, from the Idea of One Mind—so do all created things originate from this One Thing through adoption.* Following the precept "as Above, so Below," we realize that two different subjects are referred by the term "One Thing" in this rubric. The superior One Thing is God (or any man's concept of God), which created all physical reality from the Idea of his One Mind. But the inferior One Thing refers to the Arcanum, which in this interpretation is the Red Mercury (red mercuric oxide). So the Red Mercury is somehow the father of all created things, which are in this case, the other arcana.

How can this be? The key is in the dropping of the word adaptation in favor of the word adoption. The author of this version of the Emerald Tablet interpreted this word to mean the taking of a child as one's own. Pulvis Solaris was seen as the child of the Red Mercury. It took on the characteristics of red mercuric oxide. Antimony was also the child of the Red Mercury and actually possessed some of the characteristics of mercury. Iron, sulphuric acid, sodium carbonate, sodium nitrate, and Liquor Hepatis were all seen as sons and daughters of the One Thing, the Red Mercury.

The third rubric states: *Its father is the Sun, its mother the Moon. The Wind carries it in its belly, its nurse is the Earth.* The red Sun (masculine aspect of God) is the father of the Red Mercury. The sun changes from a blazing red at sunrise or sunset to the yellow golden orb of midday. The red Sun carries the essence of gold, just as it is carried by his son, the Red Mercury.

The silvery Moon (feminine aspect of God) is the mother of Mercury. In the same way that the Sun was considered the father of Gold, so was the Moon thought to be the mother of Silver and Mercury, which was seen as liquid silver (quicksilver).

The mother of the Red Mercury was the Wind, the red vapor that appears during the birth of red mercuric oxide. The father of Mercury (as quicksilver) was the earth, from which it was gathered.

The fourth rubric describes the chemical process for the creation of red mercuric oxide. When mercury is mixed with Acid of Saltpeter (nitric acid), a thick red vapor is formed over the acid, and red crystals collect on the bottom. This precipitate is red mercuric oxide, which is removed from the flask and dried. The dried crystals are rubbed with quicksilver and heated once more. The remaining quicksilver and red crystals are separated, and the crystals ground to a fine powder.

This is the Red Mercury, which is considered the father of all the other arcana. Its power is perfected when it is turned into Earth (the solid crystals). Fire is the transforming nature of the nitric acid. The Subtle is the free-flowing quicksilver at the beginning of the experiment, and the Gross is the spent quicksilver at the end of the experiment. The remainder of this rubric then reads: Separate the precipitated crystals from the nitric acid solution in the first part of the experiment, then separate the subtle quicksilver from the gross quicksilver in the second part of the experiment.

The final part of the fourth rubric describes an essential part of the process, when the Red Mercury expresses itself as the red vapor above and the red precipitate below: *It rises from the Earth to Heaven, and falls back again to Earth, thereby containing within itself the powers of the Above and the Below.* Twice (both in Heaven and on Earth) have the powers of quicksilver been incorporated into the Red Mercury. The first was by mixing quicksilver in the warm acid, and the second was by rubbing the resulting solids with quicksilver and heating again.

The first part of the fifth rubric discusses the attainment of gold: *Thus will you obtain the glory of the entire Universe....* Gold was thought of as the highest expression of the metals. In earlier versions of the Tabula, the implication was that man might someday become the highest expression of nature. The rubric continues: *This is the greatest strength of all, because it conquers every subtle thing and penetrates every solid thing.* The "greatest strength" spoken of here is of course the Red Mercury. The Red Powder of Transformation conquers every subtle thing and penetrates every solid thing. In other words, it overcomes every metaphysical or psychological influence, and it infuses and perfects matter of all types.

In this way was the Universe created, states the sixth rubric. This refers back to the second rubric. In the same way that God created the universe, so does the Red Mercury transform matter. The wonders which proceed from this are elaborated in the fifth rubric. They include not only the making of gold, but the perfection of man.

The seventh rubric presents the three-fold mystery of Hermes. But Hermes is now Mercury and his tri-form nature is represented first by Quicksilver, next by the Red Mercury, and finally by Gold. Furthermore, with this third revision of the Emerald Tablet, we now have the complete Truth intended by its original author, Hermes. These three revisions with their individual interpretations provide the true understanding of the whole Universe.

In the eighth rubric, Hermes states that what he has had to say about the operation of the Sun is complete. The operation of the Sun is nothing less than the spiritual unfolding of the Universe. It shows itself not only in the maturing of all metals into gold, but in the evolution of the heavenly bodies, as well as in the perfection of the human soul. Everything in the universe is really part of the divine art of making gold.

By changing the numerology of the *Tabula* to the number eight, it was necessary to do something which was unthinkable to earlier alchemists. Namely, the arcanum Liquor Hepatis was split into its two constituent compounds: ammonia and sulphur. Also, sodium nitrate came to be identified with the properties of nitric acid, from which it arose. Now there were eight arcana: sulphuric acid, Iron, Sodium Carbonate, Sodium Nitrate (as Nitric Acid), Red Pulvis Solaris, and Black Pulvis Solaris, Ammonia, and sulphur.

In the Second Alexandrian Period, probably within fifty years of the Third Revision, a slight modification appeared. Alchemists came to see the Red Pulvis Solaris at the head of the arcana, instead of just the Red Mercury. Remember that Red Pulvis Solaris consisted of the Red Mercury (red mercuric oxide) mixed with sulphur auratum. This reddish powder was now seen as the transmuting agent sought by the alchemists.

The substitution made little difference in the previous Metaphysical Interpretation. In the third rubric, its father is sulphur (the Sun) and its mother is Mercury (the Moon). Because of the similarities in the formation of red mercuric oxide and sulphur auratum, the fourth rubric can be interpreted as referring to both compounds. The remaining rubrics can be interpreted by simply substituting Red Pulvis Solaris for the term Red Mercury.

These modifications reflected changes in the alchemical description of matter caused by the addition of the eighth arcanum (sulphur). The alchemists came to see the importance of sulphur throughout the hermetic philosophy and elevated it to a new position. All metals were assumed to be made up of two hypothetical elements, called Mercury and sulphur. The mother of metals was now seen as Mercury, and the father was sulphur. Gold was the perfect marriage of Mercury and sulphur. Other metals were corrupt and therefore became corroded.

The intimate connection between sulphur and mercury was consummated within the earth. It was believed that when red sulphur came into contact with quicksilver in the bowels of the earth, gold was the result. Similarly, white sulphur and quicksilver produced silver within the earth. Therefore, the only difference between silver and gold was whether its sulphur was white or red.

The holy marriage of the Sun and the Moon, as sulphur and Mercury, produced the Philosopher's Stone. The idea was always present in the behavior of mercury, which tends to clump together with some powders and form amalgams with many other metals. Thus the coagulating nature of mercury was easily extended to include the idea that it formed a Stone, which could be used like a touchstone to transmute metals into gold. The Stone could also be dissolved in a solution, which became known as the Elixir or Tincture. The Elixir had the same properties as the Stone and was considered a medicine to cure defects in metals or in man.

The Third Revision encouraged the Philosopher's Stone concept by formulating the agent of change as the child of the marriage of sulphur and Mercury. In the mind of alchemists, the child of such a marriage had to be an amalgam or Stone. The Egyptian alchemists foreshadowed the idea of a magical stone in their beliefs about the formation of bezoars in the intestines of animals and men. Capturing the essence of Liquor Hepatis in a thick balsam also demonstrated the concept of solidifying a spiritual presence.

The Emerald Tablet, that ancient green stone said to be part of creation itself, is really the original Stone of the Philosophers. It stems from a time when the whole world attempted to agree on one philosophy. Its solidified wisdom contains the Secrets of the Ages.

Some of those secrets have been revealed in this book, but hidden within the properties of the arcana are still many secrets waiting to be discovered. The potential of some alchemical preparations has been demonstrated at the bedsides of my own patients, but there are formidable healing powers still latent in the compounds of mercury, sulphur, sodium, and iron.

We must start back on the road from whence we came and rediscover the lost knowledge of our Alexandrian forefathers. We must once again attempt to build one world with one true philosophy. Alchemy is that one philosophy of nature and God that can unify all our sciences, religions, and politics. Let us begin now with the art of healing. The time has come to acknowledge the alchemical foundations of medicine and to accept the Caduceus for what it is—the Staff of Hermes!

For a Complete List of Publications,
Please address:
Holmes Publishing Group
Postal Box 2370
Sequim WA 98382 USA